Mother
to
TIGERS

*S*uppose you were a lion cub—abandoned.
Suppose you lay hungry and cold
in the straw at the back of the den,

and a man came in the cage
and lifted you into a case

and put you in a car
to go home with him.

Suppose a woman bathed you.
Suppose she warmed milk on the stove
and poured it in a bottle
and put you on a pillow in her lap
to drink till you were full and sleepy,

then put you in a box that would be your bed
in a kitchen that would be your home

till you got big enough to roam the apartment,
stalking the sofa, pouncing on the chairs,
till you outgrew a human's house
and went home to the Bronx Zoo.

Your name would be MacArthur,
and the woman who saved you,
Helen Frances Theresa Delaney Martini.

GEORGE ELLA LYON

Mother to TIGERS

Illustrations by

PETER
CATALANOTTO

❖

A RICHARD JACKSON BOOK
ATHENEUM BOOKS *for* YOUNG READERS
NEW YORK LONDON TORONTO SYDNEY SINGAPORE

Helen never planned to raise cubs.
She and her husband, Fred, wanted children.
But their first baby died,
and doctors said she couldn't have more.

To ease their hurt hearts,
they collected pets: a parrot, a dog,
a starling, and twelve canaries.

Before long, their little apartment
was full of song and feathers.

On weekends, when Fred was free
from his job as a jeweler,
they strolled through the Bronx Zoo,
just down the street from their house.

Fred loved those times—
watching polar bears dive
and elephants amble,
studying the grace of giraffes.
Finally Helen said,
"Why don't you follow your heart
and work at the Zoo?"
So he did.

Each night he brought home questions
about animals he cared for,
and together he and Helen would read and learn.

When he brought MacArthur home
to the apartment on Old Kingsbridge Road,
the cub was a pitiful sight.
"Just do for him what you would do
for a human baby," Fred told Helen.
And she did.

After MacArthur
came Dacca, Rajpur, and Raniganj,
a litter of Bengal tigers.

Rajpur was so cold and thin,
Helen thought he might die,
but she put him on a heating pad
and sat by him for hours
moistening his mouth with milk.
At last he gave a weak cry.
Helen almost cried too.

Feeding three was a challenge!
Helen wished she were an octopus.
But before long those scrawny babies
were sleek, fat cubs, ready to romp.

Once, washing clothes in the bath,
Helen heard Raniganj crying.
His head was caught behind a pipe.
While she ran to the rescue,

Rajpur and Dacca discovered the tub.
Crouch . . . leap . . . *splash!*
Tigers love water.

When the striped trio
had to go back to the Zoo,
they still needed their bottles,
so Helen brought a hot plate
and set up a little kitchen
in the sleeping room
at the back of their cage.

The first night, she and Fred
ate their dinner there too.
Helen didn't want to leave
till her cubs were fast asleep.
Come daybreak, she was back

and she was thinking:
  These tigers will grow up,
    but there will always be zoo babies
    who need special care.
      She couldn't take all of them home,
      but she could bring home to them.
      She could start a nursery at the Zoo!

    "Just give me a room," she said
        to Mr. Crandall, the man in charge.
        "I'll do all the work."
        And she did.

      She cleaned and plastered a storeroom,
        which she painted pink and blue.

      Then she begged, borrowed, and bought
        everything she needed.

Starting out, she didn't get paid,
but that wasn't what mattered.
She was following her heart,
and her nursery filled up quickly.

Soon it was official:
She was the first woman keeper
in the history of the Bronx Zoo.

Before Helen arrived,
no tiger born at the Zoo had ever survived.
She raised twenty-seven,

along with yapoks and marmosets,
gorillas and chimpanzees,
deer and ring-tailed lemurs.

She still took cubs home, too:
lions, tigers,
jaguars, and a black leopard.

Helen's cubs had cubs
that were sent to zoos
all around the world.
The idea of the nursery spread too.

So, wherever you live,
when you go to the zoo,
look hard at the mighty cats.

Their grandparents
may have opened their eyes
on Old Kingsbridge Road,

may have learned to walk
in that apartment kitchen,

saved
by Helen Frances Theresa Delaney Martini,
mother to tigers.

Helen Frances Theresa Delaney was born on June 6, 1912, in Saint John's, Newfoundland. Her father was a merchant seaman. Because of something wrong with her eyes, doctors thought she would go blind, but Helen refused to believe it. She continued going to school with her two brothers, even when they had to walk through snowstorms.

After her father's death in 1925, Helen's mother took her to New York City, where a series of eye operations saved her sight. She became a student at Joan of Arc High School.

In 1932, Helen married Fred Martini. Fred was hired by the Bronx Zoo in 1940 and, in 1942, brought MacArthur home. In February 1944, he carried in the three tiger cubs. Word spread quickly about the woman raising tigers in her apartment, and soon photographs of Helen and her zoo babies appeared in newspapers, magazines, and newsreels.

After she began the Zoo Nursery in June 1944, the loving care she gave her baby cats was extended to everything from addaxes to yapoks. That August she was put on the payroll as the Zoo's first woman keeper. She said of her work, "Every day is just like Christmas. Anything can happen."

I first learned of Helen Martini when I was about ten years old and discovered her book, *My Zoo Family*. She wrote it for grown-ups, but I read it, fascinated by the photographs of lions and tigers playing in her apartment. I thought that when I grew up, I might be a zookeeper, too—tending animals on display, keeping them clean, fed, and healthy.

The next year, on a trip to New York, my parents took me to the Bronx Zoo in hopes that I could meet my hero. She wasn't there that day, but I was able to see some of her big cats. And, though I didn't become a zookeeper, I did marry a Lyon and raise cubs of the human variety.

Helen Martini left the Bronx Zoo in 1960. As of now, there is no marker at the zoo to remember her. But the nursery and her great-grandcubs live on.

In memory of Helen Martini (1912–1994)
and for all animal rescuers, especially
Paula Marie Bunch   —G.E.L.

For Bill Bingman, Cassie Delaney, and Cassie Donahue.
Special thanks to Steven Johnson, Diane Shapiro,
Suzanne Bolduc, and Nina Raushenberg   —P.C.

THE AUTHOR WISHES TO THANK:
Steven Johnson, librarian and archivist at the Wildlife Conservation Society,
which runs the Bronx Zoo, for his help in all aspects of the research on this book;
Robert M. McClung, curator of the Bronx Zoo's Mammal Department from
1949 to 1955 and author of many books about animals (including *Rajpur,
Last of the Bengal Tigers*), for sharing his memories of working with Helen
Martini and for reading the manuscript;
Cathryn Hilker, founder of the Cat Ambassador Program at the Cincinnati Zoo,
for an interview about her work to save big cats and a behind-the-cages tour;
Trudy LaFramboise and Rollins College Archives for sharing correspondence
(and tape!) from Martini's award and appearance there; and
Bill Leigh, of W. Colston Leigh, Inc., for sharing boyhood memories of Helen
Martini when she was one of the "speakers of substance"
the agency represented.

Atheneum Books for Young Readers
An imprint of Simon & Schuster Children's Publishing Division
1230 Avenue of the Americas   New York, New York 10020
Text copyright © 2003 by George Ella Lyon
Illustrations copyright © 2003 by Peter Catalanotto
All rights reserved, including the right of reproduction in whole or in part in any form.

Book design by Michael Nelson
The text of this book is set in Hiroshige.
The illustrations are rendered in watercolor, charcoal, and torn paper.

Manufactured in China
First Edition
10 9 8 7 6 5 4 3 2 1

LIBRARY OF CONGRESS CATALOGING-IN-PUBLICATION DATA
Lyon, George Ella, 1949–
Mother to tigers / written by George Ella Lyon.
p.   cm.
"A Richard Jackson book."
ISBN 0-689-84221-X
1. Martini, Helen—Juvenile literature.
2. Zoo keepers—United States—Juvenile literature.
[1. Martini, Helen. 2. Zoo keepers.
3. Women—Biography.] I. Title.
QL50.5 .L96 2002
590'.7'3092—dc21
[B]   00-045375